Welcome to a collection of heartfelt poems that reflect the deep, unwavering faith and creative spirit of Angel Schmid. As a young woman with a heart full of passion for both music and poetry, Angel has found a way to share her love for God and His Word through the written word, offering a message of hope, love, and grace for all who read these pages.

Angel's musical journey began with a gift from her grandpap, an acoustic guitar that sparked a lifelong connection to music. With her father, a guitarist for the renowned band FFDP, she was immersed in the world of music from an early age, singing alongside talented musicians and embracing her calling. But her true passion lies in poetry, especially poetry that speaks to the heart of her Christian faith. Through each poem, Angel channels her love for God and her desire to inspire others—especially young women navigating the challenges of life.

Angel knows firsthand that life is not always easy for young women in today's world. The pressures, the struggles, and the weight of expectations can often feel overwhelming. There have been moments when life left her curled up on her bed in tears, feeling lost and broken. At times, if it weren't for God's love and the loving embrace that only He can provide, Angel knows she would have given up many times over. But God, in His endless grace, has always been there to pick her up, wipe her tears, and set her back on her feet—or even carry her forward when she couldn't go any farther on her own. It is this deep-rooted love and faith in Christ that has provided the strength and resilience to face each day, no matter how difficult. Through every trial, God's presence has *been her anchor, offering the healing and peace she so desperately needed, and giving her the courage to press on.*

This book of poems is more than just a collection of words; it is a reflection of Angel's mission to uplift and encourage others in their own faith journeys. The funds raised from the sale of this book will go directly to funding the transformation of these poems into songs and the studio time required to record them. In this way, each poem not only brings a message of faith and inspiration to readers, but also helps bring Angel's songs to life, so others can experience her music and the powerful messages that inspired them.

In these pages, you will find poems that speak to the birth of Christ, the power of faith and trust, the beauty of nature, the power of prayer, and the struggles we face in life—all woven together with the threads of God's love. Each poem is a testament to Angel's unwavering belief in the power of God's grace and the transformative love of Christ.

As you read, may you be inspired, uplifted, and reminded of the deep love God has for you. Angel's prayer is that through these poems, you will find comfort, encouragement, and strength as you walk through life's challenges, knowing that God is always by your side.

~ Little Angel Schmid

About Angel Schmid

Angel Schmid's love for music began as a young girl when her grandpap gifted her an acoustic guitar. He started teaching her the classic "Classical Gas," inspiring her with the words, "If you can play this, you can play anything." Her singing journey unfolded naturally while spending time with her dad, the guitarist for FFDP, in the studio. Surrounded by music and talented musicians, Angel began singing along, with her first performance being "The Sound of Silence," accompanied by the band—though this cherished moment was never recorded.

Angel's faith is the cornerstone of her musical journey. Her upcoming songs, which she hopes to record and release, are all drawn from Christian-based poems she has written. Poetry is not only a passion for Angel but also a profound way for her to share her faith and the Word of God with other young women navigating life's challenges.

When Angel isn't pursuing her music and poetry, she volunteers at her church's daycare and is an active member of the youth ministry at Sheffield Family Life Center in Kansas City, Missouri. Her heart for service and her creative spirit make her a shining example of living a faith-driven life. Angel's current poetry book project reflects her mission: to inspire and uplift others while funding her journey to bring her poems to life as songs

Table of Contents

Section 1: The Birth of Christ

1. A Star to Guide Us
2. Born in a Manger
3. The Shepherd's Song
4. Mary's Joyful Heart
5. Glory to the Newborn King

Section 2: Faith and Trust

1. Walking on His Promises
2. In His Hands
3. When the Storms Come
4. Unshakable Hope
5. Trust Without Borders

Section 3: Love and Grace

1. His Love Never Fails
2. Forgiven and Free
3. Embraced by Grace
4. Love Beyond Measure
5. The Greatest Gift

Section 4: Worship and Praise

1. Lift Up Your Voice
2. Songs of the Redeemed
3. Holy, Holy, Holy
4. A Heart of Worship
5. Forever Glorified

Section 5: Prayer and Reflection

1. In the Quiet Place
2. Speak, Lord, I Am Listening
3. When Words Fail
4. The Power of Amen
5. A Soul's Deep Cry

Section 6: Creation and Nature

1. The Master's Canvas
2. His Handiwork Everywhere
3. The Whispering Trees
4. Majesty in the Skies
5. Nature's Hallelujah

Section 7: Overcoming Struggles

1. Beauty from Ashes
2. His Strength in My Weakness
3. The Valley's Song
4. Breaking Chains
5. Victorious in Christ

Section 1: The Birth of Christ

A Star to Guide Us

Beneath the velvet midnight sky,
A star was lit to shine on high.
It led the wise, the humble, the meek,
To find the Savior they did seek.

A beacon bright, a heavenly light,
Guiding all to holy sight.
With every step, their faith grew strong,
A journey of hope, where hearts belong.

Oh, star of wonder, star of grace,
Illumine the world with your embrace.
For in the glow of your radiant gleam,
Lies the truth of God's eternal dream.

~ Little Angel Schmid

Born in a Manger

Among the hay, a Child lay,
The King of Kings on this holy day.
No palace walls, no jeweled crown,
Yet heaven's glory was shining down.

The animals lowed, a soft refrain,
In the quiet of night, love's refrain.
Angels sang, their voices soared,
Proclaiming Christ, the Savior, Lord.

In humble beginnings, hope took flight,
Born to bring eternal light.
O holy Child, so pure, so mild,
Forever blessed, God's perfect child.

~ Little Angel Schmid

The Shepherd's Song

*The shepherds watched their flocks by night,
When heaven broke through with glorious light.
"Fear not," the angel's voice proclaimed,
"For unto you, a Savior is named."*

*With trembling hearts, they heard the call,
A message of peace, goodwill to all.
They left their fields, their sheep behind,
To worship the Lord, salvation to find.*

*O shepherds' hearts, so full of praise,
Your song resounds through endless days.
For you were first to kneel and see,
The Lamb of God, eternity.*

~ Little Angel Schmid

Mary's Joyful Heart

Oh Mary, mother, full of grace,
With love's pure light upon your face.
You bore the Christ, the Holy One,
God's precious gift, His only Son.

Your heart rejoiced, though burdens lay,
Upon your path in humble sway.
For in your arms, the Savior slept,
A promise kept, as angels wept.

Through faith and trust, you walked each mile,
A tender love, a gentle smile.
Blessed Mary, your soul's delight,
Shines forever in God's holy light.

~ Little Angel Schmid

Glory to the Newborn King

Angels sang in joyous throng,
"Glory to God!" their endless song.
The heavens rejoiced, the earth proclaimed,
The birth of the King, forever named.

Shepherds bowed, wise men brought gold,
The greatest story ever told.
In Bethlehem's town, on a silent night,
A Child was born to make wrongs right.

O come, let us adore Him now,
With humble hearts and heads that bow.
For Christ the Lord, our Savior, brings,
Eternal hope—the Newborn King.

~ Little Angel Schmid

Section 2: Faith and Trust

Walking on His Promises

*Through trials deep and valleys low,
His promises are all I know.
Each step I take, His hand in mine,
A love enduring, pure, divine.*

*In shadows dark, His light will shine,
A guide, a hope forever mine.
His words are true, His love secure,
In Him alone, I will endure.*

*O faith unshaken, trust so pure,
In Christ, my heart will rest assured.
For every path He walks beside,
My Lord, my Savior, and my guide.*

~ Little Angel Schmid

In His Hands

The world may shake, the storms may rise,
But peace I find beneath His skies.
For in His hands, my fears subside,
My refuge strong, my faithful guide.

Through every trial, every tear,
I feel His presence, ever near.
His hands, they hold me, firm and true,
A shelter safe, my heart's renew.

O hands of grace, O hands of might,
You lead me through the darkest night.
Forever held, forever known,
In Christ's embrace, I am His own.

~ Little Angel Schmid

When the Storms Come

When the storms of life come crashing in,
And doubt's cold whispers try to win,
I lift my eyes to heaven's throne,
And know I'll never walk alone.

His voice commands the winds to cease,
His presence brings unyielding peace.
Through every trial, every pain,
His love remains, my steadfast gain.

O Lord of mercy, Lord of grace,
You calm the seas, You set the pace.
Forever strong, forever near,
In every storm, You quell my fear.

~ Little Angel Schmid

Unshakable Hope

*Hope anchored firm within my soul,
Through Christ alone, I am made whole.
No trial too great, no pain too deep,
For in His arms, my heart will keep.*

*The cross before, the world behind,
In Him, eternal peace I find.
His promises, my guiding star,
His love has brought me from afar.*

*O hope unshakable, strong and true,
Forever found in You, my view.
For all my days, my song will be,
Hope everlasting, Christ in me.*

~ Little Angel Schmid

Trust Without Borders

Lead me, Lord, where faith abounds,
Beyond the shores, to deeper grounds.
Take my hand, I'll follow near,
Where Your love casts out all fear.

Your grace sustains, Your mercy calls,
Through oceans wide, where courage falls.
I'll trust You, Lord, with all my heart,
To walk by faith, a brand-new start.

O boundless trust, O love so wide,
Forever Yours, my soul's abide.
Take me deeper, draw me near,
To trust without a trace of fear.

~ Little Angel Schmid

Section 3: Love and Grace

His Love Never Fails

His love is a river, unyielding and true,
It floods our hearts, making all things new.
Through trials and storms, it will never depart,
A constant presence that heals every heart.

No matter the darkness, His light will prevail,
His love is steadfast, it will never fail.
Through valleys low and mountains high,
His love remains, an endless supply.

~ Little Angel Schmid

Forgiven and Free

Once bound in chains of sorrow and sin,
We found redemption through Christ within.
Forgiven and free, we rise from the past,
Our hearts restored, our peace made to last.

No more guilt, no more shame,
In Christ alone, we proclaim His name.
Forgiven and free, we stand tall,
For He has redeemed us, once and for all.

~ Little Angel Schmid

Embraced by Grace

Grace surrounds us, a warm embrace,
Filling our hearts with heavenly grace.
In our weakness, His strength is shown,
His love unshaken, we are never alone.

Embraced by grace, we stand on firm ground,
His mercy and peace are all around.
We walk in His light, unafraid and true,
For His grace surrounds us, making us new.

~ Little Angel Schmid

Love Beyond Measure

No height or depth, no length or span,
Can ever measure the love of the Lamb.
It reaches the broken, the lost and the weak,
A love so profound, words cannot speak.

Love beyond measure, unbounded and free,
A love that lasts for eternity.
In Christ's embrace, we find our place,
In His love, we are forever embraced.

~ Little Angel Schmid

The Greatest Gift

The greatest gift, the Savior's birth,
A light that shines upon the earth.
Wrapped not in riches, but in humble grace,
A child of promise, in a manger's place.

The greatest gift, this love divine,
For in Him, our souls entwine.
Through His sacrifice, we're made whole,
The greatest gift, the Savior of souls.

~ Little Angel Schmid

Section 4: Worship and Praise

Lift Up Your Voice

*Lift up your voice, O child of grace,
Sing of His love, see His face.
With every breath, His praises proclaim,
His power, His glory, His holy name.*

*Lift up your voice, make the heavens ring,
For the King of Kings, we shall sing.
In worship and praise, we find our place,
Lifting His name, seeking His face.*

~ Little Angel Schmid

Songs of the Redeemed

We sing the songs of the redeemed,
Of grace and mercy, love that gleams.
From darkness to light, we've been set free,
A song of salvation, for all to see.

The songs of the redeemed, loud and clear,
Proclaiming God's love, far and near.
With joy and gladness, we raise our voice,
For in Christ, we rejoice, we rejoice.

~ Little Angel Schmid

Holy, Holy, Holy

Holy, holy, holy, Lord of all,
We stand in awe, before Your call.
With hearts lifted high, we humbly bow,
To You, the One, who reigns now.

Holy, holy, holy, forever we sing,
The praises of the everlasting King.
In reverence we kneel, His glory to see,
Holy, holy, holy, eternally.

~ Little Angel Schmid

A Heart of Worship

With a heart of worship, we come before,
Our Lord and Savior, whom we adore.
In spirit and truth, we lift our voice,
To Him alone, we make our choice.

A heart of worship, pure and true,
We give our lives, to honor You.
In love and awe, we humbly kneel,
Our hearts, our lives, we freely yield.

~ Little Angel Schmid

The Glory of God

The glory of God, shining so bright,
Fills the earth with holy light.
In His presence, we stand amazed,
To Him, our hearts are forever praised.

The glory of God, forever displayed,
In every sunrise, every shade.
We lift our hands, we lift our hearts,
For the glory of God, forever imparts.

~ Little Angel Schmid

Section 5: Prayer and Reflection

In the Quiet Place

In the quiet place, we bow our heads,
Before the throne, where mercy spreads.
In stillness deep, His presence near,
We find His peace, we calm our fear.

In the quiet place, our hearts are still,
We seek His will, our souls to fill.
With every prayer, His love we know,
In His presence, we are made whole.

~ Little Angel Schmid

Speak, Lord, I Am Listening

Speak, Lord, I am listening,
Your voice so soft, a whispering.
In the silence, I will wait,
For Your words to guide my fate.

Speak, Lord, I am yearning to hear,
The wisdom You hold, so near.
With open ears, my heart obeys,
As You lead me through all my days.

~ Little Angel Schmid

When Words Fail

When words fail, the heart will cry,
A silent prayer to the Lord on high.
In every moment, in every sigh,
He understands, He hears our cry.

When words fail, His Spirit speaks,
In quiet prayer, His peace it seeks.
No need for words, just trust and rest,
In Him, we find our soul's true quest.

~ Little Angel Schmid

The Power of Amen

Amen, we declare, our hearts in one,
The prayer ascends, the battle won.
Through faith and trust, our hope is true,
Amen, O Lord, we worship You.

Amen, the power, the final word,
Our souls are stirred, our prayers heard.
In unity, we rise and stand,
Amen, O Lord, hold us in Your hand.

~ Little Angel Schmid

A Soul's Deep Cry

A soul's deep cry rises to the sky,
For mercy, for grace, it calls on high.
In the quiet, the heart does weep,
A longing that stirs the soul from sleep.

A soul's deep cry, a prayer so pure,
A voice that seeks the Savior's cure.
In His mercy, He hears the call,
A soul's deep cry, He answers all.

~ Little Angel Schmid

Section 6: Creation and Nature

The Master's Canvas

Upon the earth, the Master's hand,
Paints skies, and seas, and golden sand.
Each stroke a wonder, each hue divine,
A masterpiece that soars, a design so fine.

The Master's canvas, so vast, so wide,
From mountain peaks to the ocean's tide.
In every leaf and every tree,
The glory of God is plain to see.

~ Little Angel Schmid

His Handiwork Everywhere

Look around, and you will see,
His handiwork, so wild, so free.
In every sunrise, every rain,
His touch is seen, His love remains.

The trees, the flowers, the sky so blue,
All speak of Him, of what is true.
His handiwork, from earth to sky,
Reveals His glory, by and by.

~ Little Angel Schmid

The Whispering Trees

The trees stand tall, their leaves they sway,
Whispering secrets of the day.
In every rustle, in every breeze,
They speak of God, the King of Peace.

The whispering trees, their song so pure,
A voice of love, forever sure.
In their silence, we find His grace,
In every branch, we see His face.

~ Little Angel Schmid

Majesty in the Skies

Majesty in the skies above,
Shining bright with endless love.
Stars that twinkle, clouds that glide,
Declare the majesty of God's pride.

The sun that rises, the moon that gleams,
Reflect His glory, His holy beams.
Majesty in the skies we see,
A mirror of His majesty.

~ Little Angel Schmid

Nature's Hallelujah

Nature sings a hallelujah loud,
With every tree and every cloud.
The mountains rise, the oceans roar,
In praise of Him, forevermore.

Nature's hallelujah fills the air,
A song of love beyond compare.
With every creature, every leaf,
We sing of God, our soul's relief.

~ Little Angel Schmid

Section 7: Overcoming Struggles

Beauty from Ashes

From ashes, beauty shall arise,
As dawn breaks forth from darkened skies.
Through pain and loss, we find our grace,
In God's embrace, we see His face.

Beauty from ashes, a life restored,
Through Christ alone, our hearts are poured.
What once was broken, now is whole,
For He has healed our weary soul.

~ Little Angel Schmid

His Strength in My Weakness

In weakness, His strength is revealed,
A mighty power that cannot be concealed.
Through trials deep, His grace sustains,
His love and power break all chains.

His strength in my weakness, my heart's delight,
In His presence, I stand in light.
No burden too heavy, no road too steep,
For in His arms, my soul will leap.

~ Little Angel Schmid

The Valley's Song

In the valley, we sing our song,
Through darkest days, we still belong.
With every step, He holds us near,
And guides us through our deepest fear.

The valley's song, a cry of trust,
We stand on faith, in God we must.
For through the valley, we shall rise,
With hearts of joy and tear-filled eyes.

~ Little Angel Schmid

Breaking Chains

Chains of fear, chains of doubt,
Through Christ, we break them all throughout.
No longer bound, no longer chained,
In Him, we're free, no more constrained.

Breaking chains, we rise and sing,
Our hearts now free, we praise the King.
Through Jesus Christ, we are made whole,
Breaking chains that bound our soul.

~ Little Angel Schmid

Victorious in Christ

We are victorious in Christ alone,
In His power, we are fully known.
No weapon formed against us stands,
For Christ's victory is in our hands.

Victorious in Christ, our Savior and King,
His love and grace to us we bring.
With joy we shout, with hearts that soar,
We are victorious forevermore.

~ Little Angel Schmid

A Note from Angel

Dear Friends,

I want to take a moment to thank you for picking up this book and for allowing my words to speak to your heart. Every poem you've read is a piece of my soul, shared with the hope that it will uplift you, inspire you, and remind you that no matter where you are in life, you are never alone.

As a young woman, I know firsthand the challenges that life can bring. I've faced moments of joy, yes, but I've also encountered struggles that sometimes seemed too heavy to bear. There have been days when the weight of the world felt too much to carry, and I've found myself curled up in tears, asking God why. But even in my darkest moments, He has never left me. His love has been a constant source of strength, and His embrace has always been there to lift me when I felt I couldn't stand.

To all the young women out there, I want you to know that you are not alone in your struggles. I've been there too. Life is full of highs and lows, but through it all, God's love will never leave you. No matter how deep the valley or how fierce the storm, God's love remains unwavering, and His grace is always available to carry you through. When you feel weak, He is your strength. When you are lost, He is your guide. When you are broken, He is your healer. There is nothing in this world that can separate you from the love of God.

I pray that as you journey through life, you hold fast to the knowledge that God is always with you, ready to pick you up, wipe away your tears, and set you back on your feet. His love is the anchor that will never fail, and no matter what challenges you face, He is there, carrying you through.

Thank you for being a part of this journey with me. Your support means the world, and I pray that my words will continue to encourage and uplift you as you walk in faith, trust, and the love of Christ.

With all my love and gratitude,
~ Little Angel Schmid

Introduction

Welcome to a collection of heartfelt poems that reflect the deep, unwavering faith and creative spirit of Angel Schmid. These poems are written for young women who may find themselves navigating challenges in a world that is not always kind or friendly to them. Angel's desire is to share her love for God and His Word through these poems, offering a message of hope, love, and grace to those who need it most. These poems are for those that feel alone or lost in a world that only sees them as something to be used.

As an aspiring model, Angel's journey has been fraught with difficulties. She was manipulated by agents she trusted, only to realize their true priorities lay in their own financial gain. This led her into the darker side of modeling, a world that often conflicts with her Christian beliefs and values. The emotional toll was immense, leaving her feeling lost and broken. Yet, in her darkest moments, God's love became her lifeline. His unwavering grace and presence gave her the strength to endure, offering her peace and a path forward when all seemed hopeless.

Angel knows firsthand how the pressures of life can weigh heavily on young women. The struggles, compromises, and feelings of isolation can feel overwhelming. If it weren't for the unshakable love of God and the embrace of Christ, Angel knows she might have given up. Instead, she found refuge and resilience in His grace, which carried her through every trial and lifted her from despair. God's love is unconditional, and His promise to never leave or forsake her has been the anchor of her life.

This book of poems is more than just a collection of words; it is a reflection of Angel's mission to uplift and encourage others in their own faith journeys. Each poem explores the raw, personal struggles faced by those who feel the world pushing them into compromises that go against their beliefs and values. These are poems for those who have felt alone in their convictions yet have found strength in God's unending love. The poems delve into moments of despair, the pain of manipulation, and the powerful redemption and peace found in Christ's loving embrace.

In these pages, you will find poems that speak to the strength, love, and unwavering presence of God when the world feels against you. Each poem is a testament to Angel's belief in the transformative power of God's grace and the hope He offers to all who trust in Him.

As you read, may you be inspired, uplifted, and reminded of the deep love God has for you. Angel's prayer is that through these poems, you will find comfort, encouragement, and strength as you walk through life's challenges, knowing that God will never leave or forsake you and that His love is unconditional.

~ Little Angel Schmid

About Angel Schmid

Angel Schmid's journey into the world of modeling began with a dream to express herself creatively and pursue a career in the spotlight. However, her path took an unexpected turn as she navigated the complexities of the industry. Early in her career, Angel was manipulated by agents she trusted, only to discover that their priorities were driven by financial gain rather than her well-being. This experience led her into the darker side of modeling, a world that often conflicted with her Christian beliefs and values. The emotional toll was immense, and Angel found herself feeling lost, broken, and disconnected from her true self.

Yet, in the midst of her struggles, Angel found solace and strength in her faith. Through God's unwavering love and grace, she was able to rise above the challenges of the modeling world and reclaim her sense of purpose. This journey of self-discovery and healing inspired her to pursue a new mission—one that combines her love for music, poetry, and faith.

From a young age, music played a significant role in Angel's life. Gifted an acoustic guitar by her grandpap, she was inspired to learn the classic "Classical Gas," with his words, "If you can play this, you can play anything," fueling her love for music. She further honed her musical skills while spending time in the studio with her dad, the guitarist for FFDP. Surrounded by talented musicians, Angel's love for music blossomed as she began singing, with her first performance being "The Sound of Silence," accompanied by the band.

Her musical journey has remained deeply intertwined with her faith. Angel's upcoming songs are all based on Christian-based poems she has written, offering a powerful outlet for her to share her love for God and His Word. Her poetry reflects her personal struggles, offering a message of hope, love, and grace to young women navigating life's challenges. Through her music, Angel seeks to provide a sense of peace and encouragement for those who feel lost or used by the world.

While modeling remains a part of her life, Angel is now focused on using her platform to inspire and uplift others through her art. Her mission is to share her personal story, encourage those who feel lost or used by the world, and offer a message of strength through faith and creativity.

Section 1: Faith and Trust

1. The Moment I Was Lost
2. When the World Fell Silent
3. Unshaken in His Grace
4. The Unseen Path
5. Grace Beyond My Doubts

Section 2: Love and Grace
6. When Love Found Me
7. A Broken Vessel Restored
8. In His Embrace
9. More Than Enough
10. The Healer of My Heart

Section 3: Worship and Praise
11. Praise Through the Pain
12. In the Shadow of His Wings
13. Songs of Redemption
14. Forever My Savior
15. Hallelujah in the Dark

Section 4: Prayer and Reflection
16. A Whisper in the Storm
17. Prayers of the Broken
18. The Comfort of His Presence
19. His Strength in My Weakness
20. A Heart Reborn in Prayer

Section 5: Creation and Nature
21. The Quiet of His Creation
22. The Stillness That Speaks
23. Witness to His Glory
24. The Beauty in the Broken
25. Grace in Every Sunrise

Section 6: Overcoming Struggles
26. The Strength to Rise
27. When I Had Nothing Left
28. Through the Valley of Shadows
29. Falling, but Never Alone
30. Unshakable, Undeniable Love

1. The Moment I Was Lost
I was lost in the noise of the world,
Chasing dreams that weren't meant to be mine.
I wore a mask, pretending to fit,
But inside, I was crumbling, out of time.

The whispers of doubt filled my ears,
A never-ending echo of fear.
I reached for things that didn't last,
Desperately hoping I'd escape my past.

But in the stillness, I heard a voice,
A gentle call, a reason to rejoice.
It wasn't in the things I had sought,
But in the love that God had brought.

He found me when I couldn't find myself,
His love became my strength, my health.
In His arms, I was never lost,
For He paid the ultimate cost.

2. When the World Fell Silent

When the world fell silent,
I felt my heart break open wide.
The noise and chaos all around,
Couldn't fill the emptiness inside.

I looked for answers in places unknown,
Searching for love in places I'd grown.
But all I found was hurt and despair,
A tangled mess, a burden too much to bear.

Then, in the quiet, He spoke my name,
A voice so soft, it put all else to shame.
It filled the void, calmed the storm,
A love that healed, made me whole and warm.

When the world fell silent, I wasn't alone,
For in His love, I found my home.

3. Unshaken in His Grace

I've stumbled, I've fallen, I've lost my way,
But God's grace has always led me to stay.
Through the highs and the lows, through the darkest night,
His love is my strength, my guiding light.

When the world tried to break me,
And I thought I couldn't stand,
His grace lifted me higher,
With a love that understands.

I am unshaken in His arms,
Held steady through all alarms.
For when I thought I was weak,
His love made me strong, gave me the courage to speak.

I stand firm, no longer afraid,
For in His grace, my fears fade.

---

4. The Unseen Path

There's a path that's hidden,
A road that I can't see,
But I know it leads to peace and hope,
A place where I am free.

I've walked through darkness, through pain and doubt,
But He showed me the way, led me out.
Though the world's distractions may call my name,
I trust in His plan, I'm not the same.

The path may be unseen, but I follow His light,
For He holds my hand through every fight.
In His love, I am strong and free,
The unseen path is where I'm meant to be.

I walk with faith, step by step,
For He's already made the way, so I'll accept.

5. Grace Beyond My Doubts

I've questioned, I've wondered, I've doubted the truth,
Could God really love me, a heart so bruised?
I've wondered if I'm too broken, too far gone,
But His love whispers, "You're never alone."

In every moment of fear and doubt,
His grace shines through, clearing the clouds.
When I feel unworthy, ashamed of my past,
His love reminds me it's never too fast.

He takes my doubts, turns them to trust,
He turns my ashes to beauty, as only He must.
In His grace, I find my peace,
Beyond my doubts, I find release.

His love is stronger than all my fears,
Grace beyond my doubts, wiping away my tears.

6. When Love Found Me

I searched for love in places unknown,
Hoping someone would call me their own.
But in the depths of loneliness,
I only found emptiness.

I thought love was in the words they said,
In promises made, but never led.
Until one day, when love found me,
Not in the world, but on bended knee.

It wasn't the love I thought I knew,
But a love so pure, so deeply true.
It healed my heart and made me whole,
A love that lives deep in my soul.

When love found me, it set me free,
A love that was always meant to be.

7. A Broken Vessel Restored

I was shattered, a vessel cracked,
Wounds too deep, I couldn't look back.
My spirit broken, torn apart,
Lost in the chaos of my heart.

But God, with His gentle hands,
Picked up the pieces, helped me stand.
He restored my soul, made me whole,
Filling the cracks, healing my soul.

Where once was despair, now hope remains,
The brokenness washed away by His grace.
I am no longer defined by my past,
For in His love, I am free at last.

A broken vessel, once lost, now restored,
In His love, I find my reward.

---

8. In His Embrace

When the world grew cold,
And I couldn't find my way,
I ran into His arms,
Where I knew I'd safely stay.

He didn't ask for perfection,
Only my heart, bruised and bare,
He held me close in silence,
And whispered, "I'm always here."

In His embrace, I found my peace,
In His love, my soul's release.
The burdens I carried, He took away,
In His arms, I'm safe today.

When I am lost, I run to Him,
For in His embrace, I'm found again.

9. More Than Enough

I thought I needed more,
More things, more love, more dreams,
But the more I searched, the less I found,
The more I realized it wasn't what it seemed.

I had it all, yet felt so empty,
Like something was missing, like I couldn't see.
Then one day, I found the truth,
That God's love was all I ever needed to soothe.

He is more than enough, more than I ever knew,
His love fills the void, makes all things new.
In His grace, I have all I need,
A love so pure, it sets me free.

I am whole in Him, more than enough,
For His love is all I'll ever trust.

10. The Healer of My Heart

I wore my scars like a heavy cloak,
A mask that hid the pain I spoke.
But no one saw the hurt inside,
The brokenness I could never hide.

Then He came, with gentle hands,
Healing wounds no one understands.
With every touch, my heart grew whole,
He healed the cracks deep in my soul.

No longer lost, no longer torn,
In His love, I was reborn.
The healer of my heart, He set me free,
Now I'm whole, just as I'm meant to be.

He heals the hurt, He makes me new,
The healer of my heart, forever true.

11. Praise Through the Pain

I didn't know how to praise,
Through the pain, through the haze.
The hurt was too much to bear,
Yet He whispered, "I'm always there."

I lifted my hands in faith, unsure,
And found that His love was the cure.
Through the tears, through the strife,
Praise became the song of my life.

The pain may linger, but so does He,
Praise through the storm, His love sets me free.
With every struggle, I will stand tall,
For in His love, I have it all.

Praise through the pain, His love is near,
In His presence, I have no fear.

12. In the Shadow of His Wings

When the world became too much,
And I felt I couldn't cope,
I found shelter in His wings,
A place of peace, a place of hope.

In the shadow of His love, I rest,
No longer burdened, no longer stressed.
His wings shield me from the storm,
In His embrace, I am reborn.

When life feels heavy, and I can't go on,
I take refuge in Him, where I belong.
In the shadow of His wings, I find my peace,
In His love, my worries cease.

Protected, loved, I am safe today,
In His shadow, I'll always stay.

---

13. Songs of Redemption

I sing a song of redemption,
A melody of grace,
A song that speaks of freedom,
Found in His embrace.

My voice was once broken,
But now it's filled with light,
For God has redeemed me,
And turned my dark into bright.

Each note is a story,
Of how I was saved,
A song that lifts me higher,
From the world that once enslaved.

Songs of redemption, they rise within,
A chorus of grace, forgiveness from sin.
My heart is free, my soul is clear,
In His redemption, I have no fear.

---

14. Forever My Savior

When the world falls away,
And everything fades,
I'll stand firm in the truth,
That His love never sways.

Forever my Savior, my refuge, my guide,
In His love, I find a place to hide.
No matter the storm, no matter the fight,
He'll lead me through, He'll bring me light.

When all else fails, He will remain,
Forever my Savior, He heals my pain.
I stand with confidence, knowing He's true,
Forever my Savior, forever new.

15. Hallelujah in the Dark

*In the darkest moments, when I could not see,
I lifted my voice, I cried out, "Set me free!"
Though the night was long and filled with fear,
God's love whispered, "I'm always here."*

*Hallelujah in the dark, I will sing,
For even in the night, He is my King.
Through the silence, through the tears,
His love is stronger than all my fears.*

*Hallelujah, a song of grace,
In the darkest times, I seek His face.
With every breath, I will sing His name,
Hallelujah, forever the same.*

16. A Whisper in the Storm
When the winds were howling,
And the world seemed so loud,
I heard a whisper in the storm,
A voice so soft, yet proud.

It wasn't in the chaos,
Or the noise of the fight,
But in the stillness, I found peace,
A love that brought me light.

His whisper calms my storm inside,
His love is where I'll always hide.
When the world is raging, I stand tall,
For His whisper is stronger than it all.

---

17. Prayers of the Broken

I've prayed through tears, through pain,
Through moments I couldn't explain.
In the quiet of my broken soul,
I found a God who made me whole.

My prayers may have been simple,
Just words of longing and doubt,
But He listened, He answered,
And He lifted me out.

Prayers of the broken, prayers of grace,
In His arms, I found my place.
He hears every cry, every plea,
For in my brokenness, He sets me free.

---

18. The Comfort of His Presence

*In the stillness, I find peace,
In His presence, all fears cease.
When the world is too much to bear,
I take comfort in His loving care.*

*No need for words, no need to speak,
His presence makes me strong, not weak.
In His arms, I find my rest,
For with Him, I am truly blessed.*

*The comfort of His presence is all I need,
For in His love, my soul is freed.
I walk through life with Him by my side,
In His presence, I will always hide.*

---

19. His Strength in My Weakness

I've felt weak, like I couldn't go on,
But in my weakness, His strength shone.
When I thought I was too broken to rise,
His love opened my eyes.

He doesn't ask for perfection,
Just my heart, bruised and worn.
In my weakness, He made me strong,
His love was with me all along.

His strength is perfect in my need,
In my weakness, He meets my plea.
He lifts me up, He makes me whole,
His love strengthens my soul.

---

20. A Heart Reborn in Prayer

I prayed with a heart full of doubt,
Wondering if God would hear me out.
But He listened, He understood,
And in His love, He made me good.

A heart reborn in prayer's embrace,
A love that fills, a peace that stays.
I no longer wonder, no longer fear,
For in my prayers, He is always near.

A heart reborn, full of grace,
With every prayer, I seek His face.
His love fills me, makes me whole,
A heart renewed, restored, and bold.

21. The Light in My Darkness

When the night seemed too long,
And shadows filled my soul,
I wondered if I'd ever find
A way to make me whole.

But in the silence of the dark,
A light began to shine,
God's love illuminated the path,
And suddenly, I was fine.

He is the light in my darkness,
The hope that leads me through,
No matter how deep the night,
His love will make me new.

In the darkest of moments,
His light is always near,
A beacon in the storm,
To calm my every fear.

---

22. Redeemed by Grace

I thought I was beyond repair,
A life so broken, hard to bear.
Mistakes that haunted every night,
I couldn't find a way to make it right.

But then His grace came rushing in,
A love so pure, it healed my sin.
No longer bound by guilt or shame,
In His arms, I found my name.

Redeemed by grace, I stand today,
No longer lost, I've found my way.
His love has lifted all my pain,
In His grace, I'll forever remain.

23. The Strength to Rise

I fell so many times before,
Weak and weary to the core.
The world knocked me down, time and again,
Until I didn't know if I could rise again.

But God, He whispered through the night,
"Lift your head, I'll be your light."
With each word, I found my strength,
A strength that carries me at length.

The strength to rise is found in Him,
When my heart is broken and dim.
With His love, I find my way,
The strength to rise, come what may.

---

24. The Healer of My Soul

My soul was heavy, full of pain,
A heart that longed to break the chain.
I searched for peace in places wide,
But found no solace on the outside.

Then He came, the Healer, true,
And washed me clean, made me new.
He touched my heart, healed every scar,
And showed me love, no matter how far.

The Healer of my soul, He knows,
The deepest hurt, the pain that grows.
In His love, I am restored,
For in His grace, I am adored.

---

25. Unbroken by the World

The world tried to mold me,
To make me what I'm not.
It told me I was broken,
But it didn't know what I've got.

I am unbroken in His love,
Stronger than I ever thought.
Though the world may push me down,
In God's grace, I wear no crown.

I stand firm, my heart aglow,
With His love, I will always grow.
Unbroken by the world's demands,
For I am held by God's own hands.

---

26. Clinging to His Promises

When the world feels shaky,
And the storms rage on,
I cling to His promises,
Like a light before the dawn.

He promised He would never leave,
That He would always be near,
In every trial, in every grief,
He whispers, "I'm here, my dear."

Clinging to His promises, I stand,
For in His word, I find my land.
His promises are sure, forever true,
In His love, I am made new.

27. God's Plan, Not Mine

I thought I knew what was best,
I made my plans, I took my test.
But every road I chose to take,
Led me down paths of heartache.

Then God stepped in, with gentle hands,
He guided me to better lands.
His plan was greater than my own,
A plan that made my heart His throne.

I trust His plan, though I don't see,
For His ways are the way to be.
His love guides me day by day,
God's plan, not mine, lights the way.

---

28. Resting in His Love

I've spent my life running fast,
Chasing dreams that never last.
I've worked so hard to prove my worth,
And in the end, felt lost on earth.

But in His love, I find my rest,
In His embrace, I am truly blessed.
No need to chase, no need to strive,
For in His love, I'm fully alive.

Resting in His love, I find my peace,
A love that never fails, never ceases.
In His arms, I am set free,
Resting in His love, eternally.

29. A Love Like No Other

I searched for love in all the wrong places,
Chasing after fleeting embraces.
But nothing filled the void inside,
Nothing could quiet my heart's cry.

Then He came, with a love so deep,
A love that stirred my soul to keep.
His love, unchanging, ever true,
A love that makes me new.

A love like no other, He offers me,
A love that sets my spirit free.
In His arms, I find my worth,
A love that gives me peace on earth.

---

30. The Beauty of Grace

I was lost, broken, and ashamed,
Filled with guilt, carrying blame.
But in His grace, I found my way,
A love that washed the pain away.

His grace is beauty, pure and true,
A love that made all things new.
It's not what I've done or earned,
But the grace in which I've learned.

The beauty of grace is all I need,
In His love, I'm freed indeed.
No more shame, no more fear,
For in His grace, I draw near.

A Note from Angel

Dear Young Women,

I want to take a moment to speak directly to you—from my heart to yours. These poems are not just words on a page; they are pieces of my journey, reflections of struggles and triumphs, and above all, a reminder that you are not alone. I know how it feels to be lost, to face challenges that seem impossible to overcome, and to feel like the world is pushing you into places that don't align with who you truly are. But I want you to hear this: God sees you, God loves you, and He will never leave you.

I've walked through dark days, and I've been where you are, feeling broken and used. But through it all, I've learned something incredibly powerful—when you have nothing left, when the world has left you feeling empty, God is there. His love is not conditional. His grace does not depend on what you've done or where you've been. His love is simply, and beautifully, unconditional. And it's that love that has carried me, lifted me, and brought me to the place where I can now share my heart with you.

You are not alone in this journey. I see you, I hear you, and I'm reaching out to you with compassion and love. As you read these words, know that I stand with you, just as God does, ready to walk beside you through whatever comes your way. His love is constant, and it's in this love that you will find the strength to rise, the courage to continue, and the peace to keep moving forward.

No matter what you're facing, you are worthy of love, you are worthy of peace, and you are worthy of all the good things God has planned for you. My prayer for you is that you always remember this truth: God's love will never fail you, and neither will I.

With all my love,
Little Angel Schmid

Printed in Great Britain
by Amazon